Duckling and kitten

Holstein cow

Mallard duck and ducklings

farm animals

Laaren Brown

Domestic goat

how to use this book

Look for these colorful tabs to guide your Animal Bites adventure.

where they live Explore different animal habitats and ecosystems

percheron horse When you see a tab this color, get a close-up look at amazing animals

how they live Learn how animals behave and adapt to their environment

vista See awesome photos that show the places animals live

big data Find the facts and figures

animal gallery Take a look at animal similarities and differences

living/working Find out different ways people interact with animals and their habitats

Just like me
Look for this feature to see how animals behave and live like humans.

table of contents

Out of doors

Many farm animals spend lots of time outdoors. To stay healthy and happy, grazing animals need wide-open countryside where they can nibble grasses and wander freely.

Home on the range

Some cattle live on huge farms called ranches. In the western United States and Canada, large herds of cattle are tended by cowhands and ranchers.

Out to pasture

Pastures are full of grasses that horses like to eat. They will pick and choose the tastiest bits. Horses are hardy and can stay outside in cold weather.

Thirsty business

All farm animals need fresh water. Farmers set up large watering tanks, or troughs, so the animals can have a drink of water whenever they like.

Going green

Sheep spend a lot of time outdoors grazing in meadows. They eat an all-salad diet that includes grass, clover, and other plants. They can spend up to seven hours a day eating.

Playtime!

Many children like to spend time outside, just as animals do. Do you like to play in a field or backyard?

7

Life in the barn

The barn is at the heart of any farm. It is the place where many of the animals sleep and eat. The barnyard is a busy place.

Right on

Jersey cows are just the right size for a small farm—about 4 feet tall at the shoulder. Their milk is high in fat. It's good for making ice cream and cheese.

The best of both

An Orpington chicken is a good egg layer, and it's friendly, too. These birds enjoy time with people.

Little piggies

Pigs use their snouts—the nose and mouth area—to sniff out tasty treats in the barnyard. Like us, pigs are omnivores. That means we eat all kinds of food, including meat and plants.

Keep it cool

Alpacas can take the cold, so long as they can seek shelter in a barn. They have a harder time staying comfortable in the heat, so the barns where they live are often cooled by fans.

Slip, sliding

Nubian goats don't just produce lots of rich milk, they're also very active. They like to play on rocks and slides, as these kid goats are doing.

Gentle giants

Once upon a time, Percherons carried knights and kings into battle. Today they are used for heavy work—plowing fields, pulling carriages, and hauling logs on small farms. Percherons are draft horses—big, strong, and calm. They are willing workers, and are also good riding horses.

Just like me
Many horses wear special iron horseshoes to protect their feet. Others go barefoot, if they're mostly walking on dirt or grass.

The **coat** is usually gray or black, although sometimes the color is a shade of brown or a mix of all three colors.

BESTIE-WORTHY?

[X] YES [ ] NO

Percherons are big, strong workhorses, but they are known for their sweet, gentle personalities.

INFO BITES

Name: Percheron Horse

Type of animal: Mammal

Home: Originally from France, but now found all over the world

Size: Stallions and geldings (males) are up to 19 hands high and 2,600 pounds. That's as big as a cargo trailer. Mares (females) are usually smaller.

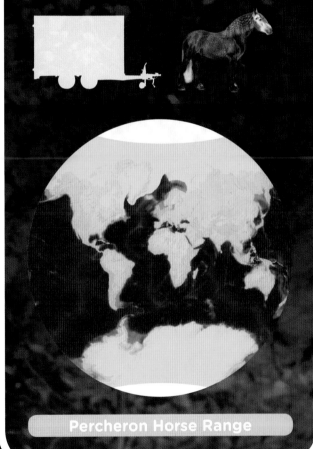

Percheron Horse Range

The **front shoulders** are called withers. A horse's height is measured in hands, from the ground to the highest point of the withers. A hand equals 4 inches.

The **fur** on the ankles is known as feathering.

Farm fresh

Every animal on the farm has to eat . . . and on a farm, the farmer makes sure everyone gets the right food (also called feed). Sometimes animals find food on their own, too.

Quacker snacks

A farmer makes sure geese have enough to eat. But geese also find tasty treats on the farm. Tender young plants in the field? A yummy snack for little goslings.

Chicken feed

Chickens eat grain and bugs, if they can get them. The birds may be fed in an open area where they can all share a feeder.

What's for lunch?

Feel like having a snack? People don't eat leaves off trees, but we eat leaves of lettuce and other veggies.

Goat goodies

Goats, like cows, are ruminants. This means they chew their food many times. After food reaches the stomach, it travels back to the mouth to be chewed again. The lump of food is called a cud. Goat stomachs have four sections to break down tough plants.

Hay is for horses

A horse can eat up to 20 pounds of hay a day, depending on its size, how active it is, and the type of hay.

Love ewe

High in the mountains of Switzerland live some of the world's most adorable sheep. These sturdy and strong sheep graze on steep, rocky slopes. Their long hair keeps them warm in the cold weather.

Short legs keep the sheep steady on steep slopes.

INFo BITES

Name: Valais Blacknose Sheep

Type of animal: Mammal

Home: The Alps in Switzerland

Size: Rams (males) are 31 inches tall and 230 pounds. Ewes (females) are 29 inches tall and 175 pounds. An upright skateboard is about as tall as these sheep.

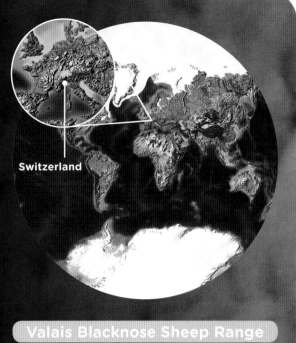

Switzerland

Valais Blacknose Sheep Range

Some **horns** are short and pointy; others spiral out from the sheep's head. Males and females both have horns.

Just like me

Every September in Furi, Switzerland, judges choose the Valais blacknose with the best hairdo. Do you like to try new hairstyles?

The **coarse wool** is often used to make carpets. Shearing takes place in the spring and fall.

SELFIE-
WORTHY?

[X] YES   [ ] NO

These sheep will make a great home screen wallpaper. Plus, their sweet nature matches their sweet looks.

All in the family

Many farm animals take family seriously. Moms take good care of their little ones. Animal dads sometimes help out, too.

Mom in charge

Scottish Highland cows are good mothers to their own youngsters—and they will also look after other cows' calves. A nudge or a push lets the young ones know when they get out of line.

Hairy care

Alpaca mothers share babysitting duty. Moms take turns supervising a group of babies, while other mothers graze farther afield.

Ram tough

Rams (dads) protect their family, and will "ram" into another animal (or person) that gets too close. Ewes (moms) keep an eye on the lambs, running after them if they wander away.

Back off, buddy!

Mother hens are very protective of their babies. They shelter chicks under their wings at night or in a rainstorm.

Taking care

Raincoat? Check. Umbrella? Check. Your parents make sure you stay dry in bad weather, too.

17

Hereford to stay

They're big. They're beefy. They're Herefords, the most common breed of cattle on earth. More than 5 million are raised around the world. Their gentle nature makes them a favorite of farmers and ranchers.

Just like me
Most Herefords have only one calf at a time, and the mothers take good care of their sweet babies.

The **tail** is used to swat away flies.

LUNCH BUDDY—WORTHY?

☐ YES ☒ No

Herefords eat about 40 pounds of food a day. That doesn't leave time for chatting.

The **coat color** is reddish brown, with a white face.

The **hornless head** on this breed makes it safer for people to work with the Hereford.

INFO BITES

Name: Hereford Cattle

Type of animal: Mammal

Home: Originally from Hereford, England, but now found all over the world

Size: Bulls (males) are about 60 inches tall and weigh 2,200 to 2,600 pounds. That's the same as an average race car. Cows (females) measure about 55 inches tall and weigh 1,300 to 1,700 pounds, the same as a small two-seater car.

Hereford Cattle Range

Four sections in the **stomach** are used to digest tough food, like grass and hay. All cattle have stomachs with four sections.

Cow country

This grass is starting on a long journey. First, a cow swallows it. Then it goes to her stomach for a little digesting. After that, it returns to the cow's mouth so she can chew it as a cud. Then back down it goes. Cow stomachs have four sections, and the food they eat visits each one in turn. This helps the cow get every bit of nutrition from her food.

Future farmers

A farm is a busy place, and young farmers have many chores to do. There are animals to feed, eggs to collect, and cows to milk. Let's get started!

Cock-a-doodle-doo

You don't need an alarm clock to wake you up on a farm—that's the rooster's job. His morning crow means "Up and at 'em— there's lots to do."

Milk, please

Cows have to be milked every morning and every afternoon. If they don't get milked, their udders become swollen and sore. Milking can be done by hand, as this girl is doing, or with milking machines.

Egg pickup

Chickens lay eggs throughout the day. On most farms, however, the eggs are collected just twice a day—in the morning and in the late afternoon.

Smarty pigs

Pigs need to be fed regularly, and they also enjoy spending time with people. Pigs are smart and are happy to play games with people and each other.

Cleaning crew

Horse stalls need to be cleaned at least once a day. "Mucking out the stall" means getting rid of poop and dirty hay.

Winter work

Farm animals that spend a lot of time outdoors grow warmer coats for colder winter weather. Farmers put on their winter coats to check on the animals when it snows.

All cooped up

A chicken coop is a little building that's made just for the chickens. When they aren't outside, the birds sleep, lay eggs, and escape the heat or cold in the coop. Most importantly, the coop provides protection from predators looking for a chicken dinner.

Chicken run

Chickens eat, peck, and scratch around in a protected outdoor area called a run.

In the nursery

These six-week-old chicks have a protected run of their own. They have a healthy supply of food and water and a soft bed of fresh greens to nibble on while they grow.

Nesting

Hens that are laying eggs use nest boxes. The boxes are dry and clean and may be lined with straw or wood shavings. Some nest boxes have openings for easy egg gathering.

Sleep tight

Chickens prefer to sleep high off the ground, where they are safe from predators. Roosting bars make the coop cozy. Day or night, hens perch together along the bar.

Tough birds

Chickens are hardy birds. Even when it's cold and snowy outside, hens will spend time outdoors hunting and pecking. Coops don't usually need to be heated.

Snug and safe

Chickens are easy prey for animals like minks, foxes, coyotes, and raccoons. They tuck themselves into tight places that predators can't reach.

Funky chicken

Many farmers keep Plymouth Rocks because they are hardy and healthy, no matter the weather. They're also gentle, and the hens take good care of their babies. A hen lays about 200 beige-colored eggs per year.

The **red comb** is small and bumpy. A chicken can't sweat. To keep cool, it loses heat through its comb.

Plymouth Rock chickens come in different colors. **Feathers** can be barred, as on this chicken, or white, light yellow, silvery, or blue.

INFO BITES

Name: Plymouth Rock Chicken

Type of animal: Bird

Home: Originally from New England, but now found in barnyards across North America and Europe

Size: Roosters (males) grow up to 9¹/₂ pounds. Hens (females) weigh up to 7¹/₂ pounds. A gallon of milk weighs about 8¹/₂ pounds.

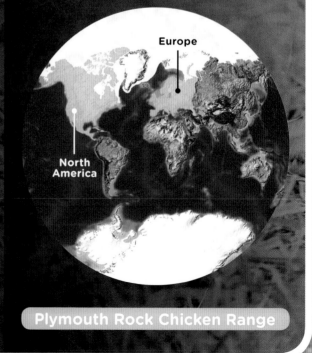

Europe

North America

Plymouth Rock Chicken Range

Wings allow the chicken to fly—a little bit. The wings are strong enough to take the bird over a fence, but not much farther.

The **stripes** on the feathers—called bars—contain less pigment than the darker areas do.

Just like me

Plymouth Rock chickens often get along with other animals. They can be best buds with the family dog.

PET-WORTHY?

☒ ☐

YES   NO

Plymouth Rock chickens can be very friendly. They even like being petted.

Sheep-a-boo!

Sheep are herd animals. That means they like to stick together—sometimes very, very close together!

Turkey trot

Look at this turkey strut. He's handsome—and he knows it. Bourbon Red turkeys were bred to be good-looking, with their deep reddish-brown coloring and white tail feathers. They are named for Bourbon County, Kentucky, which is where they come from.

Tail feathers may have reddish-brown or black stripes, called bars.

INFO BITES

Name: Bourbon Red Turkey

Type of animal: Bird

Home: Originally from Bourbon County, Kentucky, but now found on many North American farms

Size: Toms (males) weigh up to 23 pounds, about the same as a classroom desk. Hens (females) weigh about a third less.

North America

Bourbon Red Turkey Range

White feathers on the wings and tail make the turkey stand out in the barnyard.

The **wattle** turns dark red when the tom turkey is upset or is trying to impress the ladies.

WATCH-TURKEY?

[X] YES [ ] NO

Bourbon Reds are feisty. Some are like watchdogs, warning people and other animals when danger (or a mail carrier) approaches.

Just like me

Tom turkeys are sometimes called gobblers because of the sounds they make. People are called gobblers when they eat really fast.

31

Chatty chickens

Chickens may not all look alike, but they do have one thing in common—they all love to chat. They cluck, crow, and cackle.

Buff Polish

Rhode Island red

Phoenix

California quail

Goldeneye duck

Ringneck pheasant

Araucana

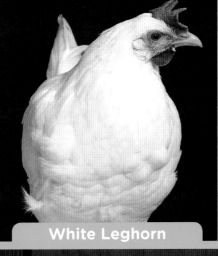
White Leghorn

Silkie

Guinea fowl

Canada goose

Wood pigeon

Feisty fowl

Fowl is another word for birds. Fowl are found on land and water, often in big groups. But not all birds are social. Some charge or bite when they feel threatened.

The stackup

TALENT: SWEET COMPANION

The Falabella is the littlest breed of horse. It originated in Argentina, South America. This smart, mini horse makes a friendly pet and companion. It can pull a cart and perform in horse shows. This horse is sometimes used as a "guide" or service animal.

TALENT: CUTENESS

The Shetland pony is small and adorable. It is easily recognized by its plump tummy and long mane and tail. It originated on the Shetland Islands, in Scotland, where it was a working breed. This pony is strong. It can pull its own weight—up to 450 pounds!

TALENT: SPOTTED EVERYWHERE!

The Appaloosa horse comes in many colors, but it is always spotted. First bred by the Nez Percé Indians of the Pacific Northwest, the Appaloosa is quick and agile. Today it is one of the most popular breeds of horse in the United States.

falabella

shetland pony

appaloosa

Up to 8 hands tall
and 70 pounds

Up to 11 hands tall
and 450 pounds

Up to 16 hands tall
and 1,100 pounds

TALENT: STYLISHNESS

The Clydesdale is a strong, heavy draft horse. This horse is equally at home pulling carts on farms, hauling lumber, or leading parades. It's named after the area of Scotland where it's from. Handsome feathering around the ankles makes it easy to identify.

TALENT: SPEEDSTER

A Thoroughbred horse can run fast over long distances and change direction easily. Thoroughbreds are the only horses that compete in the Kentucky Derby, a famous horse race. Any other type of horse would be left in the dust anyway.

TALENT: STRENGTH

Long before there were gas-powered engines for transportation and farmwork, there was the huge, strong Shire horse. In England, the Shire horse has pulled heavy loads in the fields and on the roads for hundreds of years. These easygoing horses are good for riding, too.

thoroughbred

Up to 17 hands tall and 1,000 pounds

clydesdale

Up to 18 hands tall and 2,400 pounds

shire

Up to 20½ hands tall and 2,000 pounds

Horses on the farm

Whether the animals that live there are sleek, speedy Thoroughbreds or sturdy, steady ponies, many farms revolve around the horse barn, or stable. It's the hub for resting, eating, grooming, and exercise.

Taking it easy

Horses can roam and graze in grassy pastures. They may trot around, nuzzle one another, or even roll on their backs.

A room of its own

Stalls are like bedrooms for horses. Stalls give a horse a place to rest, eat, and get ready for its next activity. The bigger the horse, the bigger the stall.

Pest control

Insects on farms can cause problems when they bite animals and people. Many bats eat insects, so they are welcome visitors on a busy farm.

In the arena

At a horse farm where people learn to ride, lessons take place in a large indoor pen, or arena. Sometimes the arena is big enough that spectators can sit and watch a riding class or a show.

Goose steps

The first breeder of these geese brought them on a "pilgrimage," or journey, across the United States. This is why they are called pilgrim geese. Today they are popular in backyard farms. A female lays 50 to 60 eggs per year. Each egg is the size of three chicken eggs.

The **wings** are good for flapping, not flying.

The **feet** are specially adapted to withstand cold winter weather.

GOOD GARDENER?

☒ YES ☐ NO

Pilgrim geese can be trained to weed the lawn. They especially like to eat dandelions.

Just like me

Geese spend time grooming themselves. They like to wash their faces in clean water.

Males have blue **eyes** and females have brown eyes.

The **bill** is smooth, without a bump.

INFO BITES

Name: Pilgrim Goose

Type of animal: Bird

Home: Native to the United States

Size: Ganders (males) weigh 12 to 14 pounds. Geese (females) weigh 10 to 13 pounds. That's the same as a can of paint.

Pilgrim Goose Range

Ooh, baby, baby

Some animals have one baby at a time, and others have two, three, or more. They all start out small and super cute.

Piglets

Baby pigs weigh about 2 to 5 pounds at birth, and they're born loving to eat and to play. When they are fully grown these piglets will weigh hundreds of pounds.

Riding high

Many young animals hang out on Mom or Dad's back. Do you like to do that, too?

Funny bunny

A baby bunny is called a kit or kitten. Its mother feeds it just once a day. The babies sleep when she's away— and when she's with them, too!

Kidding around

Baby goats are called kids. Most mother goats give birth to twins or single kids, but sometimes a mom will be surprised by as many as three babies in a litter.

Walk this way

Baby horses are called foals. Despite their long, wobbly legs, most foals can walk within an hour after they're born.

41

Long and lean

Can you guess where these cattle got their name? The horns on a Texas longhorn can be huge—up to 8 1/2 feet across.

Texas longhorns developed when wild cattle in the American West mingled with ranchers' cattle that were roaming the countryside and had babies.

INFO BITES

Name: Texas Longhorn

Type of animal: Mammal

Home: The western United States

Size: Bulls and steers (males) are 1,400 to 2,500 pounds (the weight of two sailboats), with horns 50 to 102 inches wide. Cows and heifers (females) are 600 to 1,400 pounds, with horns 40 to 84 inches wide.

Western United States

Texas Longhorn Range

Just like me

Texas longhorns use day care. In a herd, one mother will often watch over the calves while other moms graze.

The **horns** grow throughout the animal's life. Both the male and female have horns.

Long, long horns help the animal defend itself. It can also reach around to scratch itchy spots on its body.

The **body** is skinny, compared to most cattle's bodies. The meat is lean, too.

GOOD ROOMIE?

☐ YES ☒ NO

The record-holder for widest tip-to-tip horns is 109 inches. Many bedrooms are only a little bit wider.

On the go

Farmers and ranchers move their animals from place to place: to different pastures, to seasonal homes, and when taking them to market.

Taking the lead

Horses are moved to different pastures so that they always have fresh, clean grass to eat. A horse can be guided by a short lead that's similar to a dog's leash. Even a big horse will follow its leader.

Tempting treat

Moving an animal that doesn't want to budge is hard to do. Pushing or pulling doesn't usually work. But a stubborn alpaca might follow the scent of a special snack, like a slice of apple.

Keep 'em moving

Herding cattle takes teamwork. A cowhand rides in front of the herd. The herd follows the leader. Other riders bring up the rear, to make sure none of the animals wander off.

Walk this way

Pigs are smart. They are also stubborn, and it can take work to get them to move. Some may need a team of people to "herd" them the way a sheepdog does a flock of sheep. Others respond to claps and calls or can be guided with a long stick.

Lining up

Sheep naturally hang out in a group called a flock. They even stay together when they eat. Dogs help farmers watch their sheep and move them from place to place.

45

Get your goat

People have been raising goats for more than 10,000 years. Goats give us milk, meat, and soft cashmere wool. They can even pull carts. Many people think goats will eat anything—including tin cans—but they are actually picky eaters. Goats feed on grass, weeds, and other plants.

Goat **tails** are short and pointed. A goat wags its tail when it's happy.

CHEERFUL PAL?

☒ ☐
YES   NO

Goats couldn't cry even if they wanted to— they don't have tear ducts. They're happy playmates.

The **horns** are on each side of a male's head. Females often have horns, too.

INFO BITES

Name: Domestic Goat (there are more than 300 breeds)

Type of animal: Mammal

Home: All over the world

Size: Goats come in all sizes, from tiny pygmy goats that weigh just 35 pounds to big Boer goats that weigh about 250 pounds. This goat weighs about 100 pounds, the same as a toilet.

Horizontal pupils in the eyes give a wide view of the surroundings. This helps the goat spot predators.

Domestic Goat Range

Just like me

Grown-up humans have 32 teeth. So do goats. This helps them chew their food well.

Work hard, play hard

A farm is a busy place . . . the animals eat, sleep, and spend time together. But there's always time for fun.

Skippity hoppity

When lambs play in a meadow, it's called gamboling. That means happily skipping and hopping around.

Finders keepers

Many horses enjoy a fun game of tag, and a fast dog makes a good playmate.

Beautiful mud

Pigs love to wallow in mud. It helps them cool off on hot days. And they enjoy looking for tasty tidbits of food buried in the dirt.

Branching out

Goats love to climb rocks, hills, or even a seesaw in the yard. These goats, in Morocco, are climbing trees in search of food.

BFFs

Cows stay together in herds. Sometimes they will even have a best friend they like to play with.

49

Busy as a bee

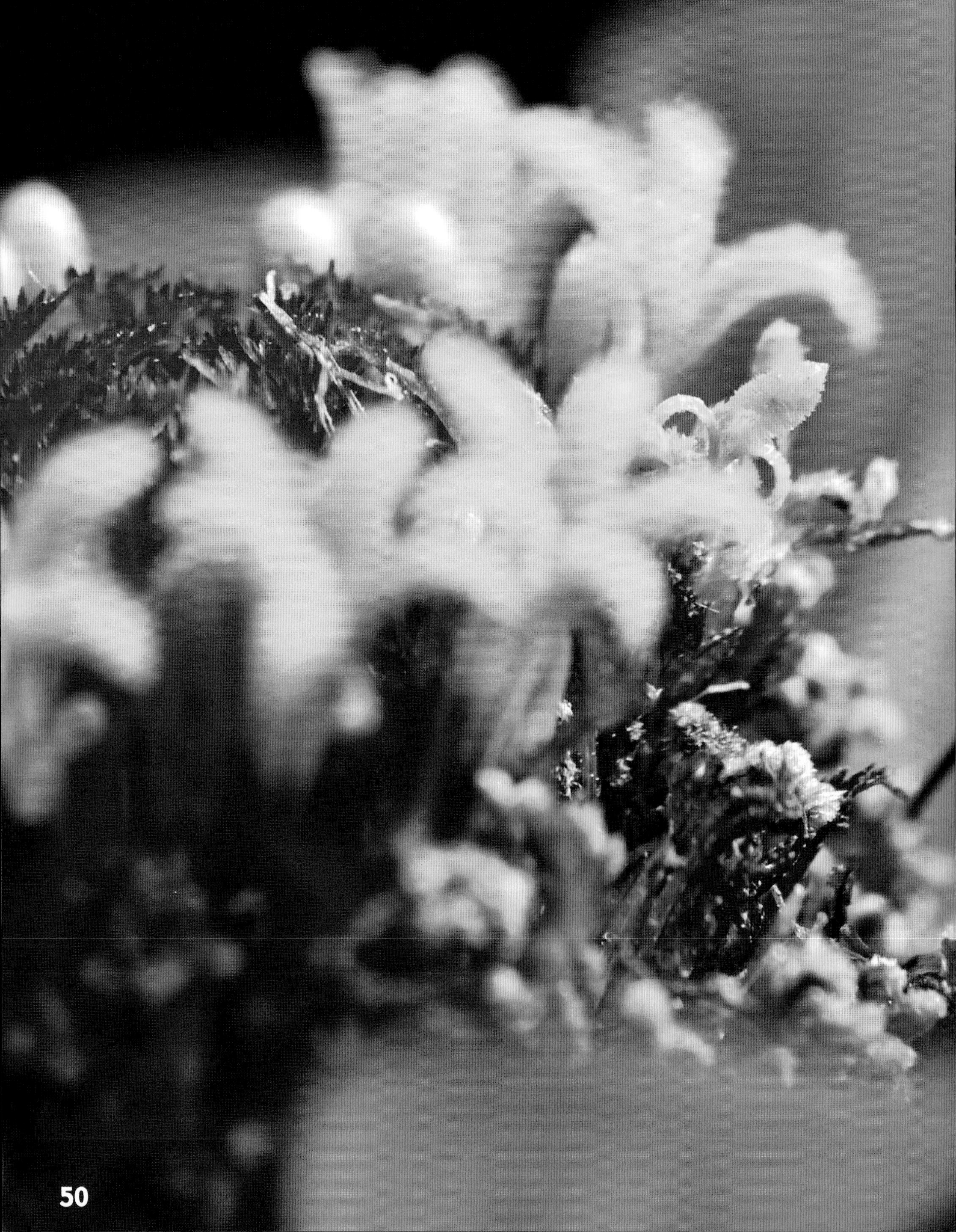

A flower, a bee, a summer day. Look closely, and it's easy to see exactly why bees are so good at pollinating whole fields of crops. They're like pollen magnets, taking some and leaving some wherever they go. Only a pollinated flower can develop into fruit, so every flower needs a visit from a bee.

This won't hurt a bit

Who keeps all the animals on the farm healthy? Veterinarians do. Vets give checkups, heal boo-boos, and help their sick patients feel better.

Listen up

A vet may listen to an animal's heartbeat. A cow's heart normally beats about 60 or 70 times per minute, about the same as a grown-up human's heart.

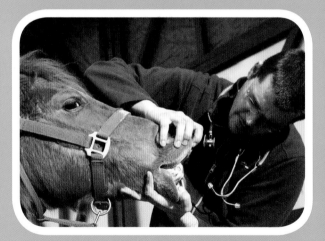

Pearly whites

Just like us, a horse can have dental problems. A vet will examine an animal's teeth to make sure they're strong and healthy.

The doctor is in

It's not easy to take a big animal to the doctor's office, so large animal vets travel to farms. They look after the health of the animals and treat problems, just the way your family doctor looks after you.

Fun at work

Squirmy piglets may make it hard for a vet to do an exam, but they make a vet's day fun.

Gear up

Instead of bringing farm animals to the doctor's office, vets bring the equipment they need to the farm. When a goat has a sore leg, it's time to take an X-ray.

53

Fuzzy face

Alpacas have lived with humans for thousands of years. They were used as pack animals by the ancient Incas of Peru. Since then, these funny faces have been raised as pack animals and for their wool. Alpacas may be vacuumed clean before their hair is sheared, or cut.

There are two types of alpaca. One, called suri, has long, silky hair. The other, called huacaya, has **curly hair**. This **curly-haired** alpaca has just had a haircut.

Just like me
Alpacas hum. It's one way they communicate with one another.

WELCOME ANYWHERE?

[X] YES [ ] NO

Alpacas are friendly and can even be house-trained. But watch out— they may spit.

The **mouth** isn't used just to eat; it's also used to spit—usually at other alpacas. The **lower teeth** grow and grow. Eating wears down the teeth, keeping them trimmed. An alpaca doesn't have upper teeth.

INFO BITES

Name: Alpaca

Type of animal: Mammal

Home: Originally from South America, but now found all over the world

Size: The average alpaca weighs 150 to 185 pounds and measures 35 inches tall at the shoulder. That's as tall as a guitar.

Alpaca Range

Helping hands

There is a lot of work to be done around a farm, so farmers can always use an extra pair of hands . . . or hooves . . . or wings. Check out these amazing animal helpers.

Pest control

Hardworking barn cats keep the farm free of mice and rats, which eat grain and other food. Just the smell of a cat will send a snake slithering away.

Lawn mowers

Sheep are happy to help out by mowing the lawn. It can take as few as three sheep to keep a half-acre of land neatly clipped.

Waste not, want not

Cows and other farm animals help keep farms clean—and prevent waste—by eating things like corn stalks, pea vines, and food scraps such as orange peels.

Besties

Horse farms sometimes keep donkeys as calming companions for Thoroughbreds. Once a donkey and horse become friends, this odd couple forms a strong bond. Goats can also be good horse companions.

Protective pal

Alpacas make excellent security guards on the farm. They watch over animals such as chickens and lambs, keeping predators at bay.

57

Border control

Got sheep? Then you need one of these. Border collies are among the smartest dogs, and they are always on the alert. These dogs live to herd sheep. Their urge to herd is so strong that in families they live with, they often keep human children in line, too.

The **ears** point up or flop down. When ears are pricked, it means the dog is listening or watching.

The **eyes** are usually brown, but sometimes they're blue. A dog may have one blue eye and one brown eye.

The **coat** is either rough or smooth. Rough border collies like this one have medium-length fur and fuzzy feathering.

Just like me

Border collies like to keep busy. They love games, mazes, and tests of agility (the ability to move quickly and easily).

INFO BITES

Name: Border Collie

Type of animal: Mammal

Home: Originally from the border between England and Scotland (that's where the *border* in the name comes from); now found all over the world

Size: Males are 19 to 22 inches at the shoulder and 30 to 45 pounds. Female are 18 to 21 inches at the shoulder and 27 to 42 pounds. A canoe is the same weight.

Border Collie Range

BFF-WORTHY?

[X] YES [ ] NO

Definitely yes. Border collies make great pets. These dogs are friendly, loyal, and full of energy.

Everyone's a winner

Farm animals may strut their stuff at a fair, a race, or another event. Animals and their owners compete to win ribbons and other prizes—and bragging rights, of course.

How now, cow?

For cattle, judges look at each animal's shape and size. They also consider how well the owner shows off the animal. The best cattle win blue ribbons.

Just like me

People test their skills in competitions, too. Do you like to run fast, jump high, or play sports?

On your mark

Pigs can really move, whether on a track or in a pool. They are surprisingly good swimmers.

Up and over

Horses compete in show jumping contests, where their riders guide them over different types of jumps.

Hopping for the best

Rabbits compete in jumping contests, too, but with bunnies they're called hopping contests. Hopping comes naturally to rabbits.

Herding help

Sheep trials are competitions for sheep-herding dogs. They test how well each dog can guide a small flock.

61

Hoofing it

The feet of hoofed animals have a hornlike covering called keratin—just like our fingernails. This helps them run over uneven ground.

Pony

Pig

Goat

Donkey

Sheep

Cow

Chick

Rabbit

Guinea pig

Cuddle up

Feathers and fur are soft to the touch, just like your favorite blanket. These animals, often found on farms, are friendly and like to cuddle.

Pig tales

This little piglet will grow up to be a not-so-little pig. Yorkshire pigs are the most popular breed of pig in North America. They are gentle and sweet. The mothers give birth to lots of piglets—often 12 in one litter—and they take good care of them.

A **long body** makes this pig look sleek, as pigs go.

The **erect ears** point up.

Just like me

Pigs are always hungry. They eat the feed the farmer gives them. They also look around for tasty treats. Do you like snacks?

BACKYARD PAL?

☐ YES ☒ NO

These pigs need shelter and lots of room to stay happy and healthy. They don't make great backyard buddies.

The **skin** is pink with dark patches, and the hair covering the body is completely white.

INFO BITES

Name: Yorkshire Pig

Type of animal: Mammal

Home: Originally from Yorkshire, England, but now found all over the world

Size: Boars (males) weigh 500 to 750 pounds. Sows (females) weigh 450 to 650 pounds. That's as much as three human dads.

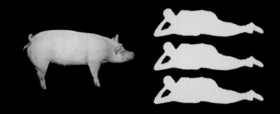

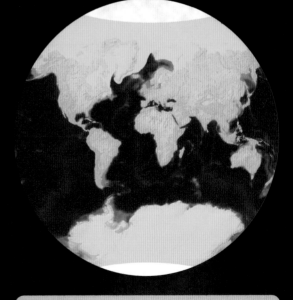

Yorkshire Pig Range

Ready, set, go!

Ducklings can swim almost as soon as they pop out of their eggs. But they can't fly until they're about eight weeks old. When it's finally time to lift off, many ducks look like they're running across the surface of the water. Then they're gone!

First meeting

How do you check out someone new? Animals use their sniffers to get information about newcomers. Scent tells animals a lot about one another.

Dog and donkey

Cat and horse

Pig and cat

Duckling and kitten

Dog and pony

Goat and sheep

Duckling and pony

Calf and pig

Chick and puppy

Horse and dog

Dog and rabbits

Pig and cat

Happy together

When animals become BFFs they act a lot like you and your friends. They play, nap, and cuddle together— and even give piggyback rides.

Friends of the farm

A working farm always has hangers-on—wild animals that benefit from the animals, crops, and people found on a farm. These animals often help the farm, too, by eating pests or pollinating crops.

We'll bee there

Squash bees are specialists. They are only interested in one kind of flower—squash blossoms. They can quickly pollinate a field of zucchini, butternut, or most other kinds of squash.

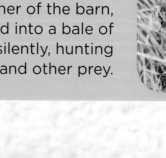

Silent hunter

The barn owl spends its days sleeping in a quiet corner of the barn, perhaps even tucked into a bale of hay. By night, it flies silently, hunting for rodents and other prey.

Happy harvest

Corn buntings don't build their nests in trees, as many birds do. They nest in farm fields, where they have a steady supply of seeds and insects to eat and feed to their babies.

In the rafters

Spiders are especially fond of farm fields and barns, where crops and animals attract tasty insects to eat.

Fast food

A barn swallow will build its nest high up in a barn, where it hunts for insects to feed its babies. This means fewer flies to bother the horses.

Gifts from the farm

Milk comes from cows . . . wool comes from sheep . . . eggs come from chickens. And that's just the start. Farm animals provide all kinds of useful things, but some really go the extra mile.

MOST MILK

The Holstein gives more milk than any other breed of cow. The average is nine gallons a day, or 3,285 gallons in a year. One record-breaker produced 8,395 gallons in a single year.

FEELING SHEEPISH

Chris the sheep was lost in the Australian outback for six years. When he was finally rescued, his

BUSY BEE

When honeybees travel from flower to flower collecting pollen and nectar, they transfer pollen to other plants. In this way, they pollinate about 80 percent of the world's plants and crops. One honeybee can pollinate 5,000 flowers a day.

EGGS-TREME

Chickens lay a lot of eggs—on average, about 250 a year. The record is held by a White Leghorn chicken that laid 371 eggs in 364 days. That's a lot of omelets!

STAYING WARM

A musk ox needs warm fur to survive the frozen Arctic. Its downy hair is the warmest fiber of all. It is about eight times warmer than sheep's wool. On musk ox farms, the fur is gathered when the animals shed their hair.

GOOD STUFF

All farm animals make at least one highly valuable product: manure. Manure contains nutrients that an animal ate, so it is good fertilizer for crops. A horse produces nearly 9 tons (18,000 pounds) of manure a year.

emergency haircut produced 89 pounds of wool—enough to make 30 sweaters.

Farm activities

RACE TO THE BARN

Ducks waddle—they sway from side-to-side as they walk. Goats like to leap and jump. Pigs walk on their toes. And sheep gambol, which means skipping and jumping. Which animal is fastest?

What you'll need:

- 2 pieces of string or rope, each about 8 feet long
- 4 players
- 1 person to call "Go" and determine the winner

1. In an open space outside or indoors, stretch out a length of rope—this will be the starting line.

2. Take twenty steps forward and stretch out the second piece of rope—this will be the "barn."

3. Decide who will move like a duck, a goat, a pig, and a sheep.

4. Line up at the starting line. When the timer calls "Go," race to the second piece of rope. Who reaches the barn first? Now switch up animals and try it again.

FLUFFY FLOCK

Make a fluffy sheep...or a whole flock!

What you'll need:

- green construction paper
- kids' school glue
- cotton balls
- black crayon or marker

1. Put a dot of glue on the paper.

2. Place a cotton ball on the glue. Press down gently on the cotton ball, to make sure it sticks.

3. Using a crayon or marker, draw the head on one side of the cotton ball. Draw four legs below.

Give your sheep some friends. Add as many sheep as you'd like to have in your flock.

SOUNDS LIKE . . . ?

Different animals make different noises. Can you match the farm animal with the sound it makes?

Animal	Sound
chicken	hee-haw
cow	gobble gobble
pig	maa
donkey	moo
horse	quack
duck	cluck
goat	neigh
sheep	oink
turkey	baa

Answers: chicken →cluck; cow →moo; pig →oink; donkey →hee-haw; horse →neigh; duck →quack; goat →maa; sheep →baa; turkey →gobble gobble

Resources

FIND OUT MORE

Continue your farm adventure and explore more amazing animals by reading more books, checking out interesting websites, visiting zoos and museums with farm exhibits, and going to working farms that welcome visitors.

PLACES TO VISIT

UNITED STATES

Los Angeles Zoo & Botanical Gardens
Los Angeles, CA
lazoo.org
Guests can see a wide range of farm animals up close at the Winnick Family Foundation Children's Zoo, part of the Los Angeles Zoo, and have a chance to interact with sheep, alpacas, rabbits, potbellied pigs, and more. Educational presentations show how these animals live and what they are like.

Smithsonian National Zoological Park
Washington, DC
nationalzoo.si.edu
Cows, donkeys, hogs, goats, and alpacas are among the animals living at the Kids' Farm at this zoo. Children can touch and even groom some of the animals. Learn what it takes to care for farm animals. Exhibits include the Cow Pasture, the Caring Corral, the Barn, and goat and miniature donkey yards.

Lincoln Park Zoo
Chicago, IL
lpzoo.org
The Farm-in-the-Zoo exhibit provides lots of opportunities for hands-on activities. There is a contact yard, where people can touch the animals. A presentation in the Dairy Barn shows how the milking process works. Meet goats, cows, chickens, pigs, ponies, and sheep.

Living History Farms
Urbandale, IA
lhf.org
Discover how farming in North America has changed through the years at authentic sites that show how farmwork was done in the past. Sites include the 1700 Ioway Indian Farm, the 1850 Pioneer Farm, and the 1900 Horse-Powered Farm. Find out, too, about modern farming practices.

Sedgwick County Zoo
Wichita, KS
scz.org
The Children's Farms at the zoo feature farms from different parts of the world: America, Asia, and Africa. The livestock living on each of these zoo farms is very different. Some of the rarest farm animals from around the world call the zoo home.

Maple Farm Sanctuary
Mendon, MA
maplefarmsanctuary.org
This sanctuary is home to about 100 rescued farm animals. Animals living at the sanctuary include chickens, goats, cows, pigs, sheep, and llamas, as well as a miniature horse. Visitors can interact with the animals and learn about them. Visits are by appointment only.

Minnesota Zoo
Apple Valley, MN
mnzoo.org
The goal of the zoo's Family Farm is for visitors to "become part of a community of people, plants, and animals striving to maintain balance with nature." See chickens, goats, horses, cows, pigs, rabbits, and sheep. Learn what these animals eat, and where and how they live.

Central Park Zoo
New York, NY
centralparkzoo.com
The Tisch Children's Zoo in Central Park is home to the only cow in Manhattan. Other animals living here include sheep, goats, and pot-bellied pigs. At the Touch Exhibit, guests can interact directly with the animal residents.

Greensboro Science Center
Greensboro, NC
greensboroscience.org
Visit the center's Friendly Farm to meet alpacas, donkeys, sheep, and goats. Guests can pet the animals in the zoo's contact yard and take part in the daily Friendly Farm feedings.

Riverbanks Zoo & Garden
Columbia, SC
riverbanks.org
Find out what lives in the barn at the Riverbanks Farm. Alpacas, Jersey cows, and barn owls are among the animals living on the farm. Feed Nubian goats in the contact ring.

Woodland Park Zoo
Seattle, WA
zoo.org
Visitors to the Family Farm can find out why farm animals are important to our lives. They get the chance to interact with donkeys, chickens, goats, sheep, and pigs. A contact area where guests can pet the animals is open in the summer.

CANADA

Oshawa Zoo and Fun Farm
Oshawa, ON
oshawazoo.ca
Animals living at the Fun Farm include goats, sheep, llamas, potbellied pigs, Texas longhorn cattle, and miniature donkeys, cattle, and horses. Visitors are able to feed and pet the residents. A number of the farm animals came to the zoo through its rescue program for orphaned animals.

Central Experimental Farm
Ottawa, ON
Friendsofthefarm.ca
A working farm located in the country's capital city of Ottawa, the Central Experimental Farm is home to the Canada Agriculture and Food Museum. The farm includes a modern dairy barn, a small animal barn, an arboretum, and ornamental gardens. Daily demonstrations provide insight into how the animals live and show different aspects of farming.

Toronto Zoo
Toronto, ON
torontozoo.com
Goats, donkeys, pigs, rabbits, and alpacas live in the Kids Zoo area. There's a water park and an interactive play area for little visitors—kids can climb into a giant spider's web and take pony rides.

BOOKS

ANIMALS: A VISUAL ENCYCLOPEDIA
Meet more than 2,500 amazing animals in this comprehensive, family-fun, global reference guide from Animal Planet—your source for all things animal. Explore the many ways animals are just like us. The book includes more than 1,000 stunning photos!

OCEAN ANIMALS
This Animal Bites book takes the reader on a journey through the oceans. Learn about marine animals from around the world, and see how and where they live.

POLAR ANIMALS
This Animal Bites book takes the reader from the tippy-top of the planet to the very bottom. Learn about the animals that call the North and South Poles home, and see how and where they live.

WILD ANIMALS
This Animal Bites book takes the reader on a journey into the habitats of wild animals around the world. Learn about animals that survive and thrive in the wild, and see how and where they live.

WEBSITES

You can visit all of the zoos and animal centers online to learn more. Here are some additional websites to check out.

climatekids.nasa.gov
Learn about animals, technology, and Earth's climate; play games; watch videos; and find crafts and activities on this informative and fun kid-friendly website from the National Aeronautics and Space Administration.

discoverykids.com
Check out some of the animals found on a farm. Play games and watch videos at this entertaining site for kids.

nationalzoo.si.edu
Take a virtual tour of the Smithsonian Institution's Kids' Farm to learn about the animals that live there and what they are like.

Glossary

arena A building used for sporting events and animal shows, with a large show area surrounded by seats.

boar An adult male pig.

bull A mature male of various species, including cattle.

breeding The process of mating and producing babies.

calf A baby cow.

chick A baby chicken.

▼ coop A building that houses chickens or other farm birds.

*Chickens eat, sleep, and lay eggs in this **coop**.*

cow A mature female of various species, including cattle.

cowhand A person who looks after cattle; a cowboy or cowgirl.

cud Grass or hay brought back up from the stomach of a cow or other animal to be chewed again.

draft horse A large horse used to pull heavy loads.

duckling A baby duck.

ewe A female sheep.

fertilizer A substance added to soil to help crops grow. Manure is a fertilizer.

flock A group of animals that lives or is kept together. Birds and sheep live in flocks.

foal A baby horse.

forage To search for food.

fowl Another name for birds.

gambol To run and skip playfully.

gander An adult male goose.

▼ gosling A baby goose

*A **gosling** has soft yellow and gray feathers.*

graze To feed on grass or other food throughout the day.

groom To clean an animal, usually a horse or a dog.

hand A unit of measurement used for the height of a horse, from the ground to the top of the withers (the shoulders). One hand equals 4 inches.

heifer A young female cow that has not had a baby.

▼ herd A group of animals that lives or is kept together. Horses live in herds.

*Horses travel in groups called **herds**.*

keratin A tough material found in nails, hair, horns, and hoofs.

kid A baby goat, or a young person.

kit A baby rabbit. Some other babies are also called kits.

lamb A baby sheep.

litter A group of baby animals born at the same time.

mammal An animal that produces milk to feed its young, has hair on its body, and has a backbone. Humans, cows, and horses are mammals.

manure Animal poop.

mare A female horse.

nectar The liquid produced by plants. It is sweet and is used by bees to make honey.

nutrient A substance that plants, animals, and people need to grow.

omnivore An animal that eats both plants and meat.

▼ paddock An enclosed area or small field where animals are kept.

Alpacas hang out in areas called **paddocks**.

pasture A field with grass grown especially for animals to eat.

piglet A baby pig.

pilgrimage A journey to a special place.

pollinate To move pollen from plant to plant, fertilizing flowers in the process.

predator An animal that hunts and eats other animals.

prey An animal that is eaten by other animals.

ram A male sheep.

ruminant An animal that has more than one stomach compartment and brings its cud back up for extra chewing. Cows and sheep are ruminants.

▼ shear To cut the wool from a sheep.

People **shear** *sheep to collect fur, called fleece.*

sow An adult female pig.

stall A walled-off area for a horse or other animal in a barn.

stallion A grown male horse that is able to father foals.

tom turkey A male turkey.

udder The part of a cow or goat that produces milk.

veterinarian A doctor for animals.

wallow To roll around in mud or water.

▼ wattle Extra skin around the head of a chicken, turkey, or other bird.

The **wattles** *on this chicken are red.*

withers A horse's shoulders.

Index

Photo credits

Key: BG – Background; CL – Clockwise from top left; TtB: Top to bottom

DT – Dreamstime.com; SS – Shutterstock.com; IS – iStock

Front Cover TtB: ©John Greim/LOOP IMAGES/Loop Images/Corbis, ©racorn/SS, ©Juice Images/Corbis, ©Jodie Coston/Getty, ©Thorsten Milse/robertharding/Corbis

Back Cover: ©Marilyn Barbone/DT

Front Endpaper: ©Carola Schubbel/DT

Back Endpaper: ©Nicole Spencer/DT

p 1: ©Tanyashir/DT; pp 2-3: ©Edwin Butter/SS; pp 4-5: ©Ana Gram/SS; pp 6-7 BG: ©Pichugin Dmitry/SS; CL: ©LifeJourneys/IS, ©FLPA/Andrew Bailey/FLPA/Superstock, ©DenisFilm/SS, ©Blue Iris/SS; pp 8-9 BG: ©Mark Hryciw/DT; CL: ©Buddy Mays/Alamy Stock Photo, ©Melissa Sanger/Getty, ©Carola Schubbel/DT, ©Tim Belyk/SS; pp 10-11 BG: ©Virgonira/DT; p 10: ©Vaclav Volrab/DT; p 11 CL: ©Kellers/DT, ©Isselee/DT, ©AridOcean/SS; pp 12-13 BG: ©northlightimages/IS; CL: ©Mahayt/DT, ©Lisa Leveck/EyeEm/Getty, ©Stanko07/DT, ©Jacek Chabraszewski/DT; pp 14-15 BG: ©S-F/SS; p 15 CL: ©Davidyoung11111/DT, ©Gradts/DT, ©AridOcean/SS; pp 16-17 BG: ©Guenter Guni/Getty; CL: ©Patryk Kosmider/SS, ©malerapaso/IS, ©Sergey Novikov/SS, ©Milosz_G/SS; pp 18-19 BG: ©JohnCarnemolla/IS; p 19 CL: ©clu/IS, ©Aubrey1/DT, ©AridOcean/SS; pp 20-21: ©George Kroll/DT; pp 22-23 Top: ©Carroteater/DT; Bottom CL: ©bouybin/SS; ©Macsim/SS, ©Margaret Miller/Getty, ©Ianych/SS, ©Patrick Heagney/IS, ©Dan70/SS; pp 24-25 BG: ©Modfos/IS; p 25 TtB: ©Leslie Banks/DT, ©cinoby/IS, ©IvonneW/IS, ©Amy Kerkemeyer/SS, ©sergioboccardo/IS; pp 26-27 BG: ©Elenathewise/DT; p 26 CL: ©Milo827/DT, ©Michiel de Wit/SS, ©AridOcean/SS; pp 28-29: ©gopause/SS; pp 30-31 BG: ©Amy McNabb; p 30 CL: ©Amcnabb3/DT, ©mphillips007/IS, ©AridOcean/SS; pp 32-33 BG: ©Luminastock/DT; 1st row LtR: ©Nicole Spencer/DT, ©Ariene Studio/SS, ©driftlessstudio/IS, ©kenneththunes/IS, ©Nicole Sharp/SS; 2nd row LtR: ©mbfotos/IS, ©Kkulikov/SS; 3rd row LtR: ©Glenn Price/SS, ©Tom Reichner/SS, ©Tom Reichner/SS, ©inkwelldodo/SS, ©Peter Zijlstra/SS; pp 34-35 1st row LtR: ©Julia Remezova/SS, ©Eric Isselee/SS, ©Eric Isselee/SS, ©Chucky/DT, ©Tamara Bauer/DT, ©Eric Isselee/SS; 2nd row LtR: ©Eric Isselee/SS,, ©Zhanghaobeibei/DT, ©Carolyne Pehora/DT; pp 36-37 BG: ©gmnicholas/IS; CL: ©Valeriy Kirsanov/DT, ©Martin Applegate/DT, ©Janina Kubik/DT, ©Brian Walter/DT; pp 38-39 BG: ©Elena Elisseeva/DT; p 39 CL: ©Charles Brutlag/DT, ©Jameswimsel/DT, ©AridOcean/SS; pp 40-41 BG: ©Grafphotogpaher/DT; CL: ©Dennis Van De Water/DT, ©Vera Zinkova/SS, ©Christy Nicholas/SS, ©Patrick Foto/SS; pp 42-43 BG: ©codyphotography/IS; p 42 CL: ©jluebowman/IS, ©George Mdivanian/DT, ©AridOcean/SS; pp 44-45 BG: ©Cynthia Baldauf/IS; CL: ©Martin Schlecht/DT, ©vandervelden/IS, ©Holly Kuchera/DT, ©Natalia Deksbakh/SS; pp 46-47 BG: ©Musat Christian/DT; p 47 CL: ©Akinshin/DT, ©Iakov Filimonov/DT, ©AridOcean/SS; pp 48-49 BG: ©Matyas Rehak/DT; CL: ©Andrew Ward/DT, ©sisqopote/SS, ©K3S/SS, ©pirita/SS; pp 50-51: ©funart/IS; pp 52-53 Top: ©Dusan Petkovic/SS; Bottom LtR: ©Melinda Nagy/DT, ©Eduardo Gonzalez Diaz/DT, ©Cckkeej/DT, ©Eduardo Gonzalez Diaz/DT; pp 54-55 BG: ©rusm/IS; CL: ©Eugene Feygin/DT, ©Parkinsonsniper/DT, ©AridOcean/SS; pp 56-57 BG: ©Mikel Martinez De Osaba/DT; CL: ©Ken Schulze/SS, ©sma1050/SS, ©Dragonika/DT, ©Chris Court/ASSOCIATED PRESS; pp 58-59 BG: ©Bigandt_Photography/DT; p 59 CL: ©Isselee/DT, ©AridOcean/SS; pp 60-61 BG: ©LAByrne/DT, ©BrandyTaylor/IS, ©AnetaPics/SS, ©clearviewstock/SS, ©Ron Harris/ASSOCIATED PRESS, ©richsearsdotcom/IS; pp 62-63 BG: ©Luminastock/DT; 1st row LtR: ©Gvictoria/DT, ©Alexander Raths/DT, ©Pavel Jakubec/DT, ©Abby Rosenberg/DT, ©Silverpineranch/DT; 2nd row LtR: ©Kelly MacDonald/SS, ©Xalanx/DT; 3rd row LtR: ©Joshua Snader/DT, ©Carola Schubbel/DT, ©Wouter Tolenaars/DT, ©Zcello/DT, ©xstockerx/SS; pp 64-65 BG: ©Volt Collection/SS; p 65 CL: ©Yobro10/DT, ©Wavebreakmedia Ltd/DT, ©AridOcean/SS; pp 66-67: ©Paul Farnfield/DT; pp 68-69 BG: ©Luminastock/DT; 1st row LtR: ©Grafphotogpaher/DT, ©Rybachka/DT, ©Rita Kochmarjova/SS, ©Salvatore Gerardi/DT, ©Nadiia Gerbish/DT; 2nd row LtR: ©Rita Kochmarjova/SS, ©Victoriia Baliura/DT; 3rd row LtR: ©Carola Schubbel/DT, ©Rita Kochmarjova/SS, ©Countrymama/DT, ©Rita Kochmarjova/SS, ©Marvolk/DT; pp 70-71 BG: ©HABY/IS; CL: ©U.S. Department of Agriculture, ©David Hosking/FLPA/Minden Pictures, ©alisbalb/IS, ©Whitcomberd/DT; pp 72-73 CL: ©Nigel Spooner/DT, ©Reinout Van Wagtendonk/DT, ©photos martYmage/SS, ©Iakov Filimonov/DT, ©Polaris/Newscom, ©szefei/SS; pp 74-75 BG: ©Jarretera/DT; p 74 TtB: ©Rita Kochmarjova/SS, ©Fluffy artwork created by and courtesy of Freddie Geppner; ©Cathy Britcliffe/IS; pp 76-77 BG: ©Jarretera/DT; 1st column: ©Leslie Banks/DT, 2nd column TtB: ©Alina Kurbiel/SS, ©Volodymyr Byrdyak/DT, 3rd column: ©bluedogroom/SS, 4th column TtB: ©Alexander Tolstykh/DT, ©Fiskness/DT; pp 78-79 BG: ©Jarretera/DT; p 80 BG: ©Jarretera/DT

ANIMAL BITES

farm animals

SCOUT BOOKS:MEDIA

Produced by Scout Books & Media Inc
President and Project Director Susan Knopf
Writer Laaren Brown
Project Manager and Editor Margaret Parrish
Assistant Editor and Photo Researcher Brittany Gialanella
Copyeditor Stephanie Engel
Researcher and Proofreader Chelsea Burris
Indexer Sarah Schott

Designer Dirk Kaufman
Prepress by Andrij Borys Associates, LLC

Advisor Jennifer Bundy
Lecturer, Animal Science Department, Iowa State University

Special thanks to the Time Inc. Books team: Margot Schupf, Anja Schmidt, Beth Sutinis, Deirdre Langeland, Georgia Morrissey, Megan Pearlman, and Stephanie Braga

Special thanks to the Discovery and Animal Planet Creative and Licensing Teams: Tracy Connor, Elizabeta Ealy, Robert Harick, Doris Miller, Sue Perez-Jackson, and Janet Tsuei

© 2016 Discovery Communications, LLC. ANIMAL PLANET™ and the logos are trademarks of Discovery Communications, LLC, used under license. All rights reserved.

LIBERTY STREET

Published by Liberty Street, an imprint of Time Inc. Books
225 Liberty Street
New York, NY 10281

LIBERTY STREET is a trademark of Time Inc.

All rights reserved. No part of this book may be reproduced in any form or by any electronic or mechanical means, including information storage and retrieval systems, without permission in writing from the publisher, except by a reviewer, who may quote brief passages in a review.

ISBN 10: 1-61893-413-9
ISBN 13: 978-1-61893-413-0

First edition, 2016

Printed and bound in China

1   TLF   16

10 9 8 7 6 5 4 3 2 1

Time Inc. Books products may be purchased for business or promotional use. For information on bulk purchases, please contact Christi Crowley in the Special Sales Department at (845) 895-9858.

To order Time Inc. Books Collector's Editions, please call (800) 327-6388, Monday through Friday, 7 a.m.–9 p.m. Central Time.

We welcome your comments and suggestions about Time Inc. Books. Please write to us at:
Time Inc. Books,
Attention: Book Editors,
P.O. Box 62310,
Tampa, FL 33662-2310

timeincbooks.com